Turn Your Computer Into a Money Machine

Learn the Fastest and Easiest Way to Make Money From Home and Grow Your Income as a Beginner

Volume 1

By

Income Mastery

competence. There are no scenarios in which the publisher or author of this book can be held responsible for any difficulties or damages that may occur to them after making the information presented here.

In addition, the information on the following pages is intended for informational purposes only and should therefore be regarded as universal. As befits its nature, it is presented without warranty with respect to its prolonged validity or provisional quality. The trademarks mentioned are made without written consent and can in no way be considered as sponsorship of the same.

Table of Contents

Introduction

"The key to success in business is to detect where the world is going and get there first. - Bill Gates

Today, society has gone through so many processes of transformation according to the development of technology that the digitization of this was something that had to be assumed. This has opened many job opportunities, to the point where it is possible to earn extra money from our homes, as they say, "appealing to a combination of talent, ingenuity and basic knowledge of the network we call the INTERNET.

In recent years, we have seen a new marketing phase. Originally, marketing efforts consisted primarily of vendors offering commodities on networks, now the Internet has almost become a "commodity" service, and much attention has been paid to this global information infrastructure to support other commercial services.

But let's be honest, who more than us, adults, young people or people with families, are the best placed to take advantage of this easily accessible tool that exists in most households. Just as we have thought that the Internet is a tool, we can also use it in our favor in the commercial aspect, when a person is in need of extra income to meet their expenses, even though you use it all day, some people do not realize the solution is in front of them.

Few people believe that "Internet Jobs" are legit, most consider them consumer scams or just a waste of time. This is wrong, internet jobs are legit and potentially there is a lot of money to be make.

That is why, in this book, we will   give you the basic tools so that their step "work" through the use of the Internet, is much easier and didactic. It is time to expand our minds and be able to see our computers as a money maker instead of seeing them as an electricity expense.,

First let's define the term "crowdsourcing" or outsourcing of tasks.

Below we see a paragraph taken from a study proposed by the ILO (International Labor Organization) "Coined in 2005 by writer Jeff Howe of Wired magazine, the term crowdsourcing, or outsourcing of tasks, refers to: The act of accepting a job that at some point was done by a certain agent (employee, independent or separate company), outsourcing it to an indefinite and generally large group of people, through an open call that is normally done over the Internet" (Howe, cited in Safire, 2009; see also Howe, 2006).

After this definition defining the subject who does work through the use of the internet and of course his computer. Why do we say that your computer can become a money-making machine?

Because while the traditional economy is in a volatile crisis, the online economy is in full expansion. That's why opting for a second or even third job online is a great way to invest your time and resources.

Before we begin to explain how you can find in your computer a way to generate income, we must be aware of what is the current employment situation in the world. In Latin America, there are more than 26 million people who are looking for a steady job, a constant income and are not able to get it.

"Although unemployment fell slightly, it is still very modest," Hugo Ñopo, coordinator of the International Labor Organization's (ILO) report El Panorama Laboral de América Latina y el Caribe 2018, told BBC Mundo.

And it is true, it dropped to 7.8% this year, within a slow recovery and a volatile scenario like the current one, between market uncertainty and political dilemmas. The study carried out by the ILO on this situation of unemployment allows us to consider the following points:

- Unemployment has a tendency to reverse in the next three years. This is something to highlight as it is always an improvement to realize that the number of unemployed workers is decreasing.

- The gender pay gap, which makes men earn 20% more than women, is also narrowing.

- There is a slight increase in the minimum wage if world economic growth continues to be met, and we are not saying it for the sake of saying, based on the projections made by the IMF, around one million new jobs would be created.

- The highest unemployment rates are found in Brazil (12.5%), Colombia (9.8%) and Costa Rica (9.7%).

- The lowest are now in Guatemala (2.8%), Mexico (3.3%) and Ecuador (4.2%).

- The unemployment rate for young people is three times higher than for adults, at 19.6%. **"One in five young people** in the region is looking for work and can't find it," says Ñopo (according to the ILO).

- More than half of the jobs are informal and result in workers being in a vulnerable condition with not even minimum protection. It is also said that self-employment is much less productive, that is, it has a lesser impact on the world economy, which it affects.

Let's take a look at the current situation by region:

Africa

In this continent only 4.5% that is in the average age of being able to work is unemployed and 60% of this has a permanent job. This does not mean that there is an efficient labor market, but that the majority of people in employment have been forced or in need of having to accept poor quality jobs, even without work insurance that can help them with any accident and without an average remuneration.

According to the studies, it has been foreseen that this "working" population will grow by more than 14 million people in a year and that the rates of economic growth would be super low enough to create an optimal working environment, that is to say, the creation of more jobs of this type, unjust and that transgress any type of minimum status for a job.

North America

- According to studies, unemployment is expected to reach its lowest level this year. 4.1% as measured. For the following year, it is quite the opposite, it is said that growth and economic activity will decline.

- Those with a primary level of education are likely to be the most affected, unlike those with higher education. As for jobs related to digital platforms, they will always take the lead because it is in full development.

Latin America and the Caribbean

- Despite perceptible economic growth, the labor force is expected to increase by only 1.4% until next year. The percentage of unemployment of each region of these continents must be in accordance with the situation of the labor market of each country.

Arab States

- In this state, the prevention rate is expected to remain at 7.3% until 2020. Workers who are considered migrants account for 41% of total employment, i.e. almost half of all workers.

Europe and Central Asia

- In this region unemployment is decreasing more and more. In the Eastern European area, they have a percentage of 0.7 per cent; in some other countries, long-term unemployment reaches no less than 40 per cent.

- In Central Asia, informality is widespread at 43 per cent. Working poverty, poor quality of work and persistent inequalities in the labor market remains worrisome.

Asia and the Pacific

- Economic growth continues, albeit at a much slower pace than in previous years. Here, regional unemployment is expected to persist until 2020, which is below the global average.

- In this continent, there is also a lack of job security measures and they are not stable as in other cases, they are not formal and they do not have any kind of stability in terms of income. Although in some cases efforts have been made to improve the area of protection, poverty rates are much higher.

Seeing all these global scenarios, opting for these jobs is the best option for an extra income or you can also work online full time. So, what does it mean for a person to opt for this kind of work?

Definitely, for anyone with the willingness to learn, to put into practice what we have self-taught and of course with the goal of getting extra money for their daily life, this is the perfect opportunity.

Of course, the difficulty is always taken into account as in any work but as you will see throughout this book, it is a matter of perseverance, perseverance and much impetus to move forward no matter how difficult the beginning.

Here are some reasons that are clearly important why people choose to have this extra job:

- Pay your rent or mortgage
- Pay your bills
- Paying debts
- Saving for retirement
- Investing for your family's future

How to dress

Having to wear an office suit, whether you're a woman or man, putting on heels or an uncomfortable suit, and being impeccable with your appearance is something you have the license to forget. You don't have to get all dressed up to start working – you can ever work in your pajamas! Because what matters is not how you're dressed, but the quality of your work.

Globalization of work

You probably will not meet people because working at home exempts you from having daily human contact with others. Your environment is only the people you live with and it doesn't go beyond them and the clients who commission you to do the work.

It depends on you if you use part of your free time or weapons a schedule so you can socialize a little and not stay in a sedentary life. It's entirely up to you. There are always benefits and odds and ends but it's definitely worth it. For a reason you did not leave your job that enslaves you 8 hours to a desk to do the same thing but at home.

Transport and economic savings

You will definitely save a lot of money that you may not feel a week, but a month and a year, that amount of money will become a considerable sum that you will save by simply eating at home. You won't need to go out to lunch at some restaurant or have some kind of craving that is considered an expense because you have food at hand in your refrigerator. Besides, as many know, there's nothing like eating at home.

With regard to transport, it can be summed up as "you save hours of being stuck in city traffic". What more could you want than to completely avoid the peak traffic hours that most workers have to go through, endure and try to drive well even though they lose more than 2 hours of their lives in a vehicle that transports them to their work center, which takes another 8 hours out of their lives, out of their day.

Put it this way, working from home sounds like the best part of life, right?

"The turnover of digital platform workers is quite high, because after micro-tasking for a while, many realize that this work does not satisfy their interests. As one respondent puts it: "Working on digital platforms is not for everyone, it requires diligence and skills to find a sufficient amount of work to make it profitable. Despite this, there is also a considerable proportion of individuals who continue to work in this modality over many years for various reasons. This paragraph was taken from research on the digital market, "digital platforms and the future of work" 2019.

Chapter 1: Basic Terms You Must Know Before Getting Started

Before starting with all the relevant information about the different ways to generate income through the Internet, we must know at least basic terms about the Internet.

Here are some of them:

DNS: Domain Name System or DNS = Domain Name System

It is a hierarchical nomenclature system for computers, services or any resource connected to the Internet or a private network. It is associated with varied information, with IP addresses and vice versa. Although the Internet only works on the basis of IP addresses, DNS allows humans to use domain names that are much simpler.

Domain: Is the name that identifies a website. All of them are different, each one has a particularity that makes it unique among the millions that are on the web. A single web server can serve multiple websites from multiple domains, but a domain can only point to one server.

Internal Link: They are the links that point to a different place within the same page. These types of links are useful on pages of large size or weight.

Cookie: These are small files that are downloaded to your computer when you browse websites. Cookies allow websites to recognize a user's browser. They do not contain or collect information.

HTTP: Hypertext Transfer Protocol = Hypertext Transfer Protocol

It is the most common protocol for exchanging information on the Web. It is the method in which web pages are transferred to a computer.

IP: Internet Protocol

IPs are unique and unrepeatable numbers that identify each of the computers connected to a network that runs the IP protocol.

SEM: Search Engine Marketing = Search Engine Marketing

Set of actions carried out to improve the positioning of a website through paid publications.

SMO: Social Media Optimization

Set of techniques and strategies that are used in Online Marketing, to achieve optimization in the use of social media.

SEO: Search Engine Optimization = Search Engine Optimization

The aim is to improve the visibility and positioning of the website in the results. This process is organic, which means it is not paid for. Later on, this term will be more explained.

Web Server

A program used to transfer web pages via the HTTP protocol. By extension, the computer where this type of software runs is called the server.

URL: Uniform resource locator =Uniform Resource Locator

Standard URLs are strings of characters with which a unique address is assigned to each of the resources available on the Internet: text, images, videos, etc.

What is SEO?

A general definition and the most accepted one is "*Search engine positioning or search engine optimization is the process of improving the visibility of a website in the organic results of different search engines. It is also common to name it by its English title, SEO (Search Engine Optimization)*".

If we talk about search engines, the first ones appeared in the 90s. Before Google appeared as the world's leading search engine, there were some who stayed on the path of development to become like this one. You have probably heard about Yahoo, this was a clear example of the above.

Then, logically people began to think what would be the most effective way to be able to have more public or their target is much larger and thus their businesses are more prosperous to be seen by more people. The answer, THE SEARCH ENGINES. It is at this moment that SEO is born, which "focuses on organic search results, i.e., what is not paid for".

There are two basic and essential factors on which these search engines are based: authority and relevance.

- **Authority** is basically the popularity of a website. The more popular it is, the more valuable information it contains. This is the factor that is most taken into account because it is based on the user experience or as it is now fashionable to call UX experience.

- **Relevance** is the relationship between a page and a given search. This is not simply that a page contains a lot of times the search term but that a search engine relies on hundreds of on-site factors to determine this.

SEO can be divided into two important groups:

- **On site**: This one worries about relevance. It makes sure that the web is optimal so that the search engine understands what is most important and gives you a result corresponding to what you expect. This group includes keyword optimization, load time, user experience, code optimization and URL formatting.
- **Off site**: This is the part of the SEO work that focuses on factors external to the website. The most important factors are the number and quality of links, social media presence, brand authority and performance in search results.

Of course, so far we have given you some basic notions of what you can find on the Internet and you have read about some terms that you do not normally hear in everyday life, but what you need is to know why you need SEO on your website and what benefits it gives you in the search to monetize your time on your computer surfing the Internet.

Why is SEO important?

The most important reason why SEO is necessary is because it makes your website more useful to both users and search engines. SEO is necessary to help search engines understand what each page is about and whether or not it is useful to users.

SEO is the best way for your users to find you through searches in which your website is relevant. These users are looking for what you offer them. The best way to reach them is through a search engine.

Doing SEO work is one of the easiest and most practical ways to earn extra income by doing a job online, from the comfort of your own home. Why? Because there are so many shops, platforms, services, etc. that are scattered in this vast digital plane, which will always want to be the first results that are found at the time of making a search with respect to your business area in the Google search engine.

Chapter 2: Tips to Succeed

Be committed to the work

Most people who start working over the Internet, have the false belief that by the simple fact of not being considered a "formal job" can work as they please, believe that perseverance and commitment is not necessary in this, as they have no "boss" to report progress or keep them supervised.

Have a defined strategy to obtain results.

By having defined a strategy, you have a process by which to guide you to move forward. You shouldn't jump from one to another just because you don't have immediate success. Think that instead of changing from one strategy to another, it is better to consider why the one you used didn't work and how to optimize it so that now if you get the expected result. Like they say, you can't give up on the first try.

Find out every time you can, never stop learning.

As we know, Internet is an infinite source of information, so we have within reach of our electronic devices the most useful tool to have a daily update. Of course, you always have to know how to distinguish between correct and real information and false information. It is therefore necessary to consider the veracity of the pages from which the information is taken.

Watch out, not everything is free, but you must keep in mind that valuable information costs. It must be seen as if it were an educational investment, a steppingstone for a broad academic training that will be productive at the moment of finding a job and that this knowledge adds a plus at the moment of recognizing it.

This is a "Continuous Training".

Accept the advice of those who have been doing this type of work for some time.

This is no ordinary job, no traditional job. So, the best way to avoid making mistakes that have already occurred some time ago is to take into account the recommendations of those we can call "experts" or people who have been immersed in this field "work" for some time, so to speak.

You should also bear in mind that, since it is not a traditional job, you cannot be sure that you will have a fixed income each month or the amount that a fixed job would give you. This type of work can be called "freelance".

Chapter 3: Internet employment options

Here, we present a small list of options that you can start to consider as to begin to dive into this world and have it as an extra entrance, since you are a beginner. From the most common to ideas a little researched in the vast world of the Internet.

Start a blog

It is true that when we talk about starting a blog, we immediately come to mind the word "bloggers", which is a very common term in our day to day. These are those people who use social networks or a website in order to communicate, entertain or even sell, always having constant communication with their "public". Even though there are a vast number of bloggers around the world, if you have writing skills and you find a way to capture the attention of the target audience you want to reach and you find a topic which is not so popular meaning there are not lots of blogs about it because if you have the same content as everyone else does,   it will be much more difficult to become popular. Blogging is a great way to make money. Of course, you need to publish regularly   and with an almost similar extension and/ or designs in each post you put in your feed.

One may think that you can simply have some profits through small business advertising, but with the evidence that we give day by day in the advertising shown by these bloggers, we realize the potential of this idea, signing with major brands such as Adidas, Puma, Nike, and so on. It allows us to get a small idea of the income that these people conceive when they sign contracts with big brands such as those mentioned above.

Having good relationships with other bloggers who come to you by recommendation can be a plus for the start of this virtual development journey. As they say, **"The key is perseverance."**

Minimum requirements:

- A computer
- Internet connection
- Good writing skills
- Good connection with your readers or followers.

Writing a book for KINDLE

If you are good at writing or have skills, this may be a very good option for you. Writing a book for Kindle which have a good hosting, you can make considerable profits by doing something you like or are born with.

There are all kinds of eBooks, science fiction, self-help, cooking, etc., but the most outstanding are those that have some kind of goal or end. These are those who talk about personal finances, self-help, diets, etc. This is a source of LIABLE INCOME; however, it involves considerable effort until your own eBooks are noticed on this platform and you can see your income increase.

One can choose to sell through this application or Apple website for a modest price that allows you to market your eBooks.

Minimum requirements:

- A computer
- An internet connection
- Good writing style
- Inspiration and perseverance to make an eBook that becomes a trend

Marketing audiobooks with a host page

This is a way to have a book which can gradually become more popular. They are even more popular than eBooks, so you must take into account the market in which you plan to develop so that your investments are also the right ones. It is said that people turn to the audiovisual when it comes to technical issues.

To begin with, we recommend that you choose to write your first eBook and see if it is popular and then turn it into an audiobook through some of the platforms available online.

Create an App

It's definitely much more laborious, much more technical and you have to have some basic knowledge about programming but it's worth it. If we look at examples like the popular game "Angry Birds" or even Facebook, we realize that at the beginning and even over the years, they became an incredible source of passive income.

However, don't forget to carry out exhaustive market research and make the appropriate analysis to find the right application for you, because creating an application means investing time and money.

Minimum requirements:

- Basic knowledge of programming.
- A computer with enough capacity to support the software.
- Be empathetic with your client's requirements.
- Take into account the needs you see in your potential customers so you can create an app that meets their expectations.

Community Manager

A digital marketing specialist or better known as a Community Manager can work remotely from home or take it as a stand-alone job. This person is in charge of managing the social networks of a business or brand that wants to be seen or have an impact with its target audience.

Now, this person must have a minimal knowledge of what skills are necessary.:

Google Analytics

This tool helps you to measure the impact of your publications on social networks, it allows you to create better content, is also shows you the posts which have more impacts your audience, what they want and what does not interest them. You can find more things about your audience through Google Analytics.

Doppler

Doppler allows you to create a list of subscribers from the first moment. It helps you generate more customers through a blog or account in a known social network.

For this you need an email marketing program like Doppler, although you have options like Mailchimp or Mailrelay that have a similar version but free.

Evernote

Evernote is incredible to be able to optimize your work or pending as a community manager. You can write down your ideas, entries, news, pending, check list, etc. It helps you not to overlook the ideas in your head and allows you to brainstorm in an easy way.

The community manager uses these tools to be able to make his work much more optimal.

> ➤ **Search engines:** search engines such as Google, Yahoo or Bing, are tools that are available to the user to find content on the topics they want. This person along with these search engines aim to successfully position the page, blog or account they manage. They carry out organic positioning (SEO) or payment (SEM) actions in their online marketing strategy.
>
> ➤ **Display advertising:** can be considered a billboard of the digital media. We are talking about ads or banners of different sizes and different formats, either with images, graphics or videos that manage to attract attention or generate more views in the project they are developing.

➢ **Email marketing**. This is one of the most basic and default tools a community manager can use. The good news is that it can still be used effectively and can be combined with other strategies such as lead nurturing. This tool can also serve you to make your own database and others, with which messages are generated in the form of catalogs, courses, newsletters, etc.

Offer your services as a freelancer through Fiverr

If you have any experience in your career or in a specific area or net knowledge but have not had the opportunity to work in a company, you can choose to use this platform.

Now, what is Fiverr? It is a platform in which you can offer your services as a writer, graphic designer, accountant, etc. from a basic price and people who require any of these services, offer you a job as a freelancer or independent, whatever you want to call it. On the other hand, you have posted notices of jobs that people need to be done as soon as possible and you can make a deal with them so that both sides win.

Of course, like any platform that wants to stand must have some way to raise funds, so this provides you as an option to pay a minimum amount of money to put as a priority or in their recommendations an ad or poster of yours about your work or what you want to find.

The minimum price is 5 dollars and can reach a price on which both parties agree.

Minimum requirements:

- You don't necessarily have to be an expert in the field in which you are going to offer your services as a freelancer, but you do have to carry out work that meets the expectations of your client.
- You always want to learn.

Here are some other platforms where you can look for work as a freelancer or freelancer. We must assume that at the time of starting in this life of freelancer you will not have many customers until you have had some customers, so again we tell you that it is a matter of perseverance and about getting recommendations from your own customers.

Here is a list of some of these portals:

- FreeLancer
- Twago
- Cloud
- Adtriboo
- GreatContent
- Textbroker
- Geniuzz

In these portals, like Fiverr, you will find work for writers, designers, programmers, producers and any other kind of work you can imagine. Consider them as a way to enter as a beginner into a market as competitive as the digital one.

If you want another way to find this type of work, it can be the forums. Find one related to the area in which you want to develop and begin to actively participate so that your name is one to which the public becomes known.

AIRBNB

This is an application that connects people who want accommodation, in most cases, to spend the night or a few days, with people who have spaces or rooms in their homes and are willing to rent them. All you have to do is enter their platform, define the space you are going to make available to customers, the price at which you are going to offer it and ready, publish it.

There are even options on this platform that allow you to have a higher income percentage. On this platform, you have the option of being a "superhost", what does this mean? It means being a host with a distinction before the users. It is a category that is accessed through recommendation of the same guest and gives you a reward of 20% more.

The same company, Airbnb, provides you with 22% more income than hosts with a basic category, why? Because the accommodation you offer may be in a tourist place and like any hotel, it increases the price for the tourist area in which you are. Another benefit is the number of visitors who perceive your ad. The Seo of your lodging has a better positioning before the view of the guests or users of this platform and a filter that helps to improve the lodgings, before the requirements of the users.

Basic requirements:

- A place where you can receive your guest.
- A comfortable and habitable space.
- Established house rules if you intend to rent a shared space.

Become a virtual assistant

What do we mean by that? Well, if you are good at organizing and optimizing your time, I think this option is the right one for you. Through a platform or web, you can organize meetings, make agendas, make reservations and through this, become a virtual assistant. Most of these people are hired by businessmen who do not feel the need to have an assistant present but someone who is in charge of organizing their day to day, who allows them to delegate and who can have a notion of what awaits them in their day to day.

Minimum requirements:

- A computer that allows you to connect immediately with the person who requires your service.
- Good internet connection.
- A program to help you handle pending appointments.
- A very good sense of efficiency.

Become an online teacher

If the first thing that comes to mind is a tutor but online, you got it right. It's the same job, but through the Internet, at a distance. What for? To be able to make things much easier, to not have to go to a language institute or extra classes and have to go through all the traffic in the city, let's face it, is the worst thing that can happen to us.

A clear example of this is UDEMY, but what is Udemy? It is one of the best-known learning platforms. You can participate as a student and at the same time give classes through this one.

In addition to being a teacher, you can choose to be a translator of texts in the languages you know or those you are aware of that you can work in. In other words, if your specialty is languages and you have the technique to be able to translate efficiently, there you have a work option. Traditionally, translators are needed to be able to transfer a physical book from one language to another, as they are still needed now but for virtual texts.

Programmer or web designer

This is a sector where every day increases the number of workers that shows that you can work without having to move physically and only with the support of online communications.

Who wouldn't like to make $40 to $70 an hour? This is the average income of a freelancer web developer in Latin America.

If you work for a company, you work for them 8 hours per day in the same project, you could be using those 8 hours more efficiently and earning more money. One of the most important reasons why a programmer decides to become independent is because he is not forced to program the hours the company expects him to work or even more (if we speak of exploitation) and also because he is able to work on projects that really interest him as previously said.

Here are some tips to make your future as a freelancer programmer as prosperous as you hope:

- Make yourself known in the industry

Most people start working by recommendation. Because someone told someone about your work that someone else just needed a programmer and you seemed like the one. This is also known as word-of-mouth recommendation, which in most cases works but if you want to see other options, you have internet search engines, paid advertising, etc. So that customers can see your work and create the need to contact you to propose a project.

- Tendering of projects:

Some websites, such as Guru.com or Scriplance, act as intermediaries between independent programmers and clients. Kind of like Fiverr but for programmers. In this case, the client must provide a job description and the programmers will propose an offer regarding the price, with which the client must negotiate. This negotiation includes topics such as the quality of the work, the offers that other programmers can make to the client, the time, etc. After this, it is agreed on a term in which both parties agree and once the project is delivered, the client qualifies and is considered as a score on your website. You must take into account that this affects your reputation and perception with other customers.

- Sale of programs or software:

Creating your own software and selling it can be a good idea. The advantage of this is that you can do it once and continue charging royalties for each time a user uses it, but as time goes by, you must make updates and get some format 2.0 or something like that. The softwares that have the most impact are those that have a practical orientation, such as budgets, calculations, organization and games.

As an extra, to make yourself known in the market and before you launch a specialized software, you can start by creating a free version of a basic program so people will use it and realize its usefulness and functionality, and after that you can offer an upgrade to a "Premium" version for those who subscribe or pay a sum of money.

Paid surveys

Do they work? A clear example of official platforms for this type of work is TIMEBUCKS.

This platform goes beyond surveys, is a rewards site that pays you to watch videos, watch fun slide shows, install applications, follow people on Instagram, among others. And the best of all, it's worldwide, so you don't have any restrictions.

Transcribe audios

If you have the keyboard skills and the patience to listen to audio repeatedly, you can opt for audio transcription. A reliable page for this type of work can be ATEXT, where you can receive up to 315€ per month for transcribing one hour of audio per day, Monday to Friday.

However, one thing you should keep in mind is the care and detail you must put to your spelling, since these transcriptions must never have any spelling or grammar errors. In addition to complying with the transcription guidelines detailed on the page so that you do not have points removed or money deducted from your payment.

Create Your Own Website or Platform

If you want to make your own website or platform, instead of opting for any of the above work as independent, which you can do from home using your computer, we recommend the following steps that we believe can serve you useful:

Choose your niche

What you should do as a first step is define well what will be your "niche market" in which you are going to develop, remember that it must be profitable and that it is to your liking (you are going to dedicate yourself entirely to this). You can start doing a market study or an MVP with which you can get an idea of the potential of your business.

Choose the digital media or tool you will use or focus on

Once you have selected the market niche which you are going to work with, you must define which is the media, digital or tool that you are going to use to transmit your message and apply strategies to be able to get the attention of your target audience.

This platform can be a YouTube channel, Instagram, a Facebook page, an online store, even a blog. A recommendation to start and have something purely yours can be a blog. In this medium, one is able to direct the traffic with respect to the visits and interactions of the public. It allows you to be much more flexible and gives you opportunities to monetize.

If you decide to start with an account within a social network, you have to take into account:

Create Original Content

This is the way you will get much more impact and difference from other accounts and your target audience will perceive it. It must show relevant content, which positions it as a reference in the field or niche in which it is developed. You can help yourself with a market study to know the topics of interest and at the same time analyze the competition that you have.

Chapter 4: Beware of Internet Fraud

So far, we have talked about the positive side of the internet, but as we know, not everything can be rosy. This is the dark side of the Internet, the side that can even swindle you if you have no knowledge of how some platforms act to get money out of you by promising me to get exorbitant sums of money, let's face it, nobody gives you anything without having anything in return. And then whoever says yes to you, IS LYING TO YOU.

Frauds and swindles do not come from the appearance of the Internet, they have been established for a long time. There are different ways of deceit and tricks in which people can take money out your bank information, numbers of your card with the promise of being able to accede to some subscription or benefit that in reality does not exist. However, with the emergence of the Internet, scams have been increasing. There are lots of t false promotions or ways of scamming because of the apparition of WhatsApp, social networks, Gmail, etc. However, there are several ways to avoid being scammed. In addition to this, there are also ways to stop scams from reaching more people who might fall into the trap. We are going to review some key points that must be taken into account in order to detect them and be able to avoid them.

Advance Payment Scams

The modus operandi is as follows, victims receive a message telling them that they will receive a large amount of money, but not without first paying a small amount of money in advance to secure that subsequent "prize". As soon as the victim makes the payment in advance, the scammer does not reappear, and you can see that the whole thing is a scam.

Charity Scams

Fake charitable organizations are created all the time, NGOs that ask you for donations to "save the planet", "to sponsor a malnourished child", "to plant more trees in the Amazon", etc. Remember they use logos of prestigious organizations. The best known are the donations they ask for in the fight against cancer, because they recognize that this is a sensitive issue that can impact many people.

False job offers

If you have already offered your resume over the Internet, either through LinkedIn or a similar platform, the scammers manage to penetrate the security barriers of some of these platforms and get your data so they end up communicating and give you a really good offer which could be good job, with an advance payment, exceptional working conditions that any person and more to one who is harmed by the current unemployment situation, will dazzle.

Software download

At some point we have received a message that explicitly asks us to download a software or an antivirus that will protect us or be useful for us. This software is better known as "scareware" and offers zero security.

It can appear through social networks, search engines, pop-ups so you must be alert to any of these occurrences and remove them, so it does not end up stealing your private information. If you download this program, they can hack your computer.

Theft of data by means of false websites

This type of scam is usually more common in the case of bank accounts. It is common that when you need to contact your bank or make a transaction on the Internet, you write the name of the bank in the search engine that you use frequently, for example, Google Chrome. Scammers create a cloned web page in which you can perform some steps of your transaction which allows them to steal your data and password. With this information, they can steal from you periodically. This is the reason why we recommended to write the link in the search bar, without the help of the search engine.

Automatic scams through your computer

What is sought in this modality is that the victim makes a deposit of pay for a program which they want to download or deposit money to gain money. Once they do, you will get an ID and the scammer will ask you for your account number to deposit the money you have earned. The program will open many advertising windows, which you will have to close because otherwise you will "damage" your computer and the money will not arrive. In this period of time, the scammer already has your personal information and you were scammed without realizing and there is obviously no prize.".

Malware-Based Phishing

This scam starts when the victim receives an email. Everything seems normal, but no. Since this, email carries a piece of malware as an attachment or downloadable file. Since you don´t realize that this email contains a virus for example, you download or open the attachment and instantly, the security barriers of your device are violated.

Nigerian Cards

This is a modality used all over the world. You've probably already heard of this modus operandi, so let's start with a synopsis of what it's all about.

It consists of giving hope to the victim saying they have an inherence which is quite substantial. The thing you need to do to claim the inheritance is pay a sum of money in order to access it. These emails are usually sent by fraudsters mainly from African countries such as Nigeria, Sierra Leone or Côte d'Ivoire.

Pharming Scam

It is the exploitation of the vulnerability in the software of the DNS servers (Domain Name System) or in the computer of the users which allows the attacker **to redirect a** domain name to a completely different machine so when the user wants to enter the name of the domain he wants, he will access the name of the scammer and therefore, as we know from the aforementioned scams, the user's private information will be stolen.

Now that you know about different types of scams, we can give you some tips to avoid them.

What can you do to avoid scams?

The information we provide on the web is becoming more and more extensive, therefore, we are becoming more and more vulnerable to infringement of our privacy rights. Despite these possible situations, there are ways to navigate and store our data on our own devices safely and risk-free.

Back up before you have a problem.

If you haven't backed up your information yet, then you should. This may help you if your information or device is stolen.

Keep in mind that if your cell phone or laptop is stolen, your information can be used against you.

Analyze the app or website in depth.

If you're up to date with the advancement of technology, you shouldn't be taken by surprise by this recommendation. It is never superfluous to take precautions when installing an application or when you see a website with links of dubious origin.

These measures will help you avoid fraudulent websites that supplant companies or people in order to steal money and data.

Be careful with your Internet connection.

We must be cautious because without realizing it by sharing the same Wi-Fi connection, "cyber thieves" may collect information from our devices, without us even noticing it. The problems that one should be aware of and that should sound like an alert to these malefactors are:

> ➢ **Reduced bandwidth**: Depending on the number of intruder devices connected and

their use of the network, they can prevent yours from connecting.

➢ **Theft of transmitted information**: Inadequate router configuration can allow an attacker to steal the information you transmit.

➢ **Direct connection to your devices**: An intruder with sufficient knowledge, aided by a security problem or in an installation without proper security, could "sneak" into the connected equipment.

➢ **Responsibility for illegal actions**: When you contract an Internet connection with a service provider, it is associated with your name, assigning you an IP address that identifies you within the Internet. Any action carried out from this IP will be associated with you.

We have given examples and different ways of Internet fraud or impersonation, which you should be on the lookout for. Now we'll give you some solutions or guidance on what you can do if you've already been a victim.

First, how to report a fraud if it was done over the Internet:

In the event that you suffer a scam or fraud, before making a formal report, what we recommend is that you gather as much evidence as possible, as well as the information you were given and the information you provided. You could present invoices, receipts, or other type of information to back up your claim that you have been scammed. Once you have all that information you can proceed to report them.,. In some countries they have a specific area for this type of scam, which conducts computer research to track them.

Chapter 5: Organization and Productivity

Here are some tips which can help you increase your organization and be more productive, because, working at home without the pressure of a boss, tends to relax us and allows us to have more distractions.

Working from home is entirely up to you. You are responsible for your schedules, breaks and goals. Obviously, it is very comfortable to work from home, but you need to be responsible.

Create your own work schedule.

An established schedule helps you to optimize your production time and reduce procrastination.

Are schedules always adhered to? Not always, but it is good to have established times to work.

Eliminates distractions.

Working at home is a lot of distractions. If it's not your pet, it's your parents, the phone, social media, etc.

When you sit down to work, silence your cell phone and look for a comfortable space to work. Sit in your dining room, your living room, your desk, a place other than your bedroom, because you can't be productive in the same space where you sleep. If you share the space in which you live, tell your roommates that you need peace and quiet because you are going to work.

Avoid sedentarism.

Working at home has its pros and cons but one thing we should always keep in mind is the side of how it affects health. You can become Sedentary. When you get used to working from home, you tend to sit in front of the computer most of the time. This is something you should avoid at all costs, take this into consideration before you set up a schedule to organize and optimize your time. If you don't have time to exercise take 5 minutes per hour to stretch,

Never stop learning. Try to be in continuous training and keep up to date with tendencies

If one does not continue to train and keep up with the industry´s tendencies the service, we provide begin to become outdated. Why? Let's imagine that a client using the "fiveer" platform asks you for a job on graphic design, but your designs look the same as they did five years ago. This client might ask for a different type of design, but you can´t fulfill it because you have not kept up to date with the new design programs for example.

You will lose a customer and a potential recommendation.

Use tools that allow you to optimize your work

The time you devote to an activity is worth money. So, the more you optimize your production time the better. Time is money, and when you work from home, it's worth even more.

Keep in mind that this is a non-traditional job. This is not a job in which you know that at the end of the month, you will get paid a full salary. In this job, no, it all depends on your productive hours.

Here are some applications or platforms that can be used to increase your productivity and help you get organized.

Trello

Trello is a tool in which you can organize your activities. You can add different stages to the activities, for example, when you start the work you can add 0%, 50% when you are halfway through, 75% and 100% when the task is completed. This will help you organize and improve your work quality and timing.

Spotify

Listening to music on Spotify or a music platform can be a way to boost your creativity. A way to make your workspace uniquely yours. There are even playlists that help increase concentration because of the soft melodies which improve your productivity.

Conclusion

A brief summary to take into consideration:

Throughout this book we have reviewed several topics; why people look for jobs in the internet and why it is a good idea to become a freelancer, we also explain that you might start with a lower salary and that it will take you some time to get used to the idea of not receiving a full salary at the end of month.

On the other hand, we defined basic terms such as SEO and SEM, we provide different tips on how to increase productivity, how to avoid distractions in the workplace, how to measure our impact in social media and search engines using Analytics. It is important to emphasize that we have also mentioned about the potential dangers of using the internet such as viruses and hackers stealing our information.

Furthermore, it is important to highlight that. That the decision to   earn money as a freelance is personal and that you do not need an 8 to 6 pm job to earn a salary. How can you earn money using the internet?

- Earn money by checking websites.
- Become a community manager.
- Learn how to transcribe from audio to text.
- Become a Language Translator.
- Freelance
- Program web pages.

- Become a virtual assistant.

In 1996, multimillionaire and co-founder of Microsoft Bill Gates in his essay "Content is King," predicted that the Internet would fill the role that radio once played many years ago as a broadcaster of job opportunities. Years later, we firmly believe he wasn't wrong.

More than 20 years have passed, and most Internet-related jobs are on the rise and will continue to do so. This type of jobs as freelancers, change the idea that you can only work from an office with a steady schedule.

It is true that there are more and more "independent workers and that companies even opt for "in-house" work, which allows workers to work from home a couple of days a week. Overall, working from home is a really good option to earn additional income or to have a flexible schedule. Beware of internet scams, use reliable webpages to get jobs as a freelancer, this will allow you to turn your computer into a money machine.

In recent years, the influence of "millennials" and the expectations they have for their jobs has influenced companies and their behavior. Most millennials, usually prefer in-house jobs instead of going to the office, having to dress in a formal attire and get up early in the morning to get to work on a fixed schedule. Nowadays, companies hire freelancers for administrative tasks such as customer support.

Some companies even believe that when it comes to hiring freelancers, they are hiring people who are more qualified and capable of adapting to their requirements. We even found statements like: "I think there is a shortage of talent. In the region, the job crisis is often associated with a lack of employment, but many companies do not find the right person with the education or knowledge to do the job they need" and so they turn to freelancers for the time they need them and it costs them much less than looking for a new worker and hiring him as a permanent staff.

As we have mentioned before, we have shared with you all the information we have collected throughout our study and observations which include safer ideas to earn money without falling into scams. We need to emphasize that it is all about perseverance and effort. At first you might not see the results you expect but remember that you will be able to get a job as a freelancer and you will get used to it. The more clients you get, the more recommendations you will have and therefore your profile as a freelancer will also grow.

Take our recommendations and highlights into consideration before you launch into this vast digital world. Increase your income working full time and part-time as a freelancer, or just work as a freelancer and have a flexible schedule. Be responsible, productive and persevere.

"Patience and perseverance have a magical effect before which difficulties disappear and obstacles vanish" (John Quincy Adams)

www.ingramcontent.com/pod-product-compliance
Lightning Source LLC
Chambersburg PA
CBHW071519210326
41597CB00018B/2818